FINANCIAL PLANNING for Young Couples

Cicely Jones and Dan Beck

IMPORTANT:

This book is for general informational purposes only, and no part of this text should be considered or relied upon as investment, tax, accounting, or legal advice. You should seek the services and advice of your own financial, tax, legal, and other applicable professionals before proceeding with any course of action. Investing involves risk, including loss of principal invested. Equitable Advisors, LLC (Equitable Financial Advisors in MI & TN) and its affiliates do not provide tax, accounting, or legal advice and make no representation as to the accuracy or completeness of any such statements, statistics, data, or opinions provided herein.

Cicely Jones (CA Insurance Lic. #: 0K81625) and Daniel Beck (CA Insurance Lic. #: 0K95318) are Financial Professionals who offer securities through Equitable Advisors, LLC (member FINRA, SIPC) (NY, NY 212-314-4600) (Equitable Financial Advisors in MI & TN), offer investment advisory products and services through Equitable Advisors, LLC, an SEC-registered investment advisor, and offer annuity and insurance products through Equitable Network, LLC (Equitable Network Insurance Agency of California, LLC in CA). Individual Financial Professionals may transact business and/or respond to inquiries only in state(s) in which they are duly and properly registered, licensed, and qualified.
NOTE: The terms "financial advisor" or "advisor" in this book are used in a general sense to describe insurance/annuity and investment sales and advisory professionals who may hold varied licensing as insurance agents, registered representatives of broker-dealers, and investment advisory representatives (IAR) of registered investment advisors, respectively. "Advisor" is not necessarily intended to refer to IAR-offered financial advisory/planning services.

AGE-4838958.1(03/23)(exp.03/26)

ISBN: 978-1-7373478-3-5

CONTENTS

CONTENTS

INTRODUCTION

CONGRATULATIONS on taking the first step towards figuring out what financial security looks like for you. Our goal in writing this book is to give young couples some ideas for how to answer big financial questions associated with life milestones like marriage, having children, new jobs, moving, the death of a loved one – and everything in between.

Everyone seems to have some friend who is a "financial guru." Some advice certainly can be helpful. Some is even crucial, such as telling someone not to give out their Social Security number to strangers over the phone. But too much advice can leave people confused, suffering from paralysis by analysis. It can be difficult to sort the wheat from the chaff as we're bombarded with "10 easy money hacks," the cookie cutter advice, and all those "get rich quick" schemes.

We are not here to tell you how you can get rich quick. We're here to help with your long-term financial stability.

We work predominantly with young couples (from their 20s through 40s). We've found that the tail end of Generation X, Millennials, and the front end of Generation Z are exposed to a lot of media about investments. This group of people has seen financial turmoil. Starting to think seriously about investing can bring up bad memories of parents saying their 401(k) went down by 50% or even having their childhood homes foreclosed on.

So many couples approach us with the same questions that Cicely had a dear friend suggest we put together some Frequently Asked Questions to help guide people. As that list grew and become extensive, we decided to turn it into a book.

As we go through this material, we will give you some basics on financial planning, identify some common goals that you can skip through if they don't resonate with you, and cover some basics of investing and risk management. We will also be telling you some stories of real-life examples with clients, but for privacy reasons, we will be changing names and some other identifying details.

These stories are meant to illustrate some of the questions and pitfalls young couples face and what causes them to seek out financial advice in the first place. They will also show how simple it can be to start the process.

Answering Life's Big Financial Questions

WHEN PEOPLE are embarrassed and feel like they should be further along on their financial goals than they are, they often try to hide details about their lives and financial situation. These individuals try to tell us what they need, for example, "I need to save $2,000 per month towards retirement if I'm ever going to retire." Or they say, "I need to have already started a college savings plan five years ago." Or "I need to invest aggressively right now if I ever want to buy a house."

When we hear something like this, we like to take a step back and ask where their conclusions are coming from. We like to understand people's belief systems and help them plan their financial futures. It may seem like someone who says these things has already done their homework in Excel, crunched the numbers, and come to an educated conclusion. We find that often isn't the case.

Cicely once had a friend, Cody, who believed that he started planning too late. Cody was divorced then started new relationship and told her that he "just started getting into this stuff." He ran some numbers and decided he needs to have $10 million by the time he's 50. She was curious about the calculations and logic involved, particularly because she doesn't subscribe to the notion that there's a magic number for retirement. So, Cicely asked him how he reached his conclusion.

Cody said that if you take $10 million and divide it by 50 years of life, he'd have about $200,000 per year. To him, that sounded like a pretty good income for him and his future spouse. This math checks out and seems true and logical if your assets are in cash and getting 0% returns. Let's say that instead, Cody assumed he stayed invested and just took a hypothetical 5% rate of return from his investments. Cody could have that exact same $200,000 per year in income from $4 million (after taxes, assuming no inflation) instead of $10 million. She then challenged him on what that budget looked in retirement: Was he planning to stay in a major metropolitan area? Travel more? Move out of the country? Was he calculating in a taxation expectation?

Now, you may be saying that if Cody can get to the $10 million, why would Cicely stop him? Less isn't more, more is more, right? If Cody can save $10 million before age 50, we think that is great. However, that plan could lead to psychological pain from being so far from his goal.

One major problem is that not being anywhere close to his $10 million goal was a daily source of agony for him that caused him to want to take big risks to find returns and turn a few thousand dollars into several million. He started following celebrity posts about alternative investments and fads. As you may guess, some days were good, but many were very stressful and did not take him closer to that end goal.

In financial planning, the first step is defining your goals and getting to their root assumptions before we even quantify them. Financial professionals can serve as facilitators and guides for these conversations.

Our Backgrounds

CICELY JONES AND DAN BECK have been financial professionals with Equitable Advisors since 2016.

Cicely started her career at 21 years old after graduating early from University of California, Santa Barbara. She got her start in the business focused on retirement planning, working with individuals just starting out on their retirement savings journey. In her first full year as an advisor, she was the top producer of a 25-person team. She expanded her business, becoming a more holistic planner by working with a wider range of clients with varying goals. In 2018, she was invited to be the first woman in 20 years within the Northern California/Hawaii office of Equitable Advisors to reach the Vice President level. She enjoyed mentoring new advisors and growing careers, but her favorite part of her role was still educating clients and doing financial planning. In January 2022, she decided to shift her focus back fully on clients. She is also pursuing her CERTIFIED FINANCIAL PLANNER™ professional certification to better support her clients, with an estimated completion date of July 2023.

Dan started out his professional career as a Navy Officer after graduating from the Naval Academy in 1999. After spending his 20s in the armed forces, he decided that he did not want to spend the rest of his life away at sea. Upon arriving home, Dan went to Harvard Business School in the class of 2009. At Harvard, he developed an interest for investing and decided that he would start a hedge fund. He ran the hedge fund Beck Investment Partners from 2011 to 2015. While running the fund, he completed his Chartered Financial Analyst designation and began teaching in the Chartered Financial Analyst review course. Dan found meaning in teaching and found that he wanted to work more personally with investors in his everyday career as well. This led him to join Equitable Advisors in 2016. Since joining Equitable Advisors, Dan has primarily worked with young families and a group affectionately referred to as HENRYs (High Earners, Not Rich Yet). He also continues to teach a course at University of San Francisco in Behavioral Finance.

Acknowledgements

We would like to thank our friends, clients, and families for supporting us through the writing process, giving their opinions and expertise, letting us use their stories, and their patience with us in taking longer than expected to release our book. A special thank you to Cicely's father, Steve, for putting in many hours and helping to make this book easily understandable to people with a non-financial background. Thank you to our compliance team taking time out of their busy schedules to support in getting this book published. We hope you enjoy it.

PART 1:

Goals-Based Financial Planning

CHAPTER 1:

Intro to Financial Planning

THE KEY TO PLANNING for your financial future is identifying what is important to you. Again, everyone is different, with varying backgrounds and visions for what they would like their lives to look like. Therefore, cookie cutter-advice does not work for everyone. In this section, we will be going through how someone can start to think about their unique financial plan.

First, you want to figure out what financial security looks like to you. What keeps you up at night?

Once you have that vision, it's your baseline for planning, your key value system. And the good news is that it is okay for it to change moving forward. Without a plan, the products and services you end up with from various financial institutions might cause you to end up at your ultimate goal, but it will likely be entirely by accident. If you have a quantified goal, you can measure your progress and make decisions to get you there, on purpose, every year. And no, we certainly do not mean by making speculative bets to get there.

Let's review some of the most common goals we see in financial planning: retirement planning/financial independence, college planning, and major purchase planning. We have already gone through some of the questions associated with retirement planning, but we will go in depth in the section on retirement planning.

For college, we want parents, parents-to-be, siblings, aunts/uncles, and grandparents to consider where they want to be able to send their student, what kind of tax treatment they want, if the student may be able to qualify for needs-based aid, if they want the student to take on loans, if the student may get a scholarship, if they may end up going to community college, and if they want to be able to pay for graduate school on top of undergrad.

For a major purchase, we want homebuyers, entrepreneurs, sailing adventurers and all those beyond to think of a few things. First off, how far away is the goal? Secondly, how much are we realistically going to need to get there? And thirdly, is the goal fluid? Are we depending on other factors or strictly our own ability to save for the goal and investment returns we can get?

The sooner we can define some basic goals and start investing towards them, the better. Do not let thinking you will never reach your goals stop you from planning for your financial future. "You only live once" is an approach that may feel good in the moment, but it can lead to your expenses always gobbling up your income. We've seen this not just with the younger generations but in many of those in their 50s and 60s who make over $500,000/year and have $10,000 in savings.

We do not believe in scarcity. We do not think that you must save 50% out of every paycheck to have any hope of retiring. We think you should have fun weekends where you do not work. We believe in true vacations. We don't dream of surgically removing all fun from people's lives and telling them to live their most frugal existence.

Personally, we enjoy our weekends and vacations, and we think you should too. Our goal here is to make financial security accessible while enjoying life today.

CHAPTER 2:
Retirement Planning

RETIREMENT PLANNING is, for many people in the United States, the single biggest financial hurdle we face. According to the National Institute on Retirement Security, 67% of Americans say the United States faces a retirement crisis. Almost two-thirds of Generation X and Millennials worry about not being financially secure in retirement[i].

In this chapter, we want to explore some of the reasons why this concern could be growing, how people should think about their retirement planning goals, and taxation options.

Income for Life

First, let us look at the past landscape of retirement for individuals, and how that's changing. In the last 90 years in the United States, many relied on a pension for their retirement. A pension is an obligation by some entity to pay out an income to an individual for that individual's entire life.

Pensions are usually calculated based on income, number of years of work, and an actuarial calculation of how long the individual is expected to live, plus some assumed adjustment for cost of living. When we ask people about their parents' retirement, many say something like, "My dad worked at the same company for 30 years and retired at 60 with a pension that he could live off of for the rest of his life." Much of the onus historically not been on the individual to provide for their own financial security in retirement.

One of the first pensions in the United States, Social Security, was invented essentially as insurance against living too long. Social Security benefits first came out in 1935 when the average life expectancy for a man was 59.9 and for a woman was 63.9[ii] . We were basically expected to drop dead once we reached what we know as retirement age today. If we happened to live too long, the government would then make sure that we did not have to eat dog food or live on the streets.

As we began to live longer, Social Security had to make some changes to remain solvent. Now, in the United States, current life expectancy is 81.65 for women and 76.61 for men[iii]. We have seen shifting targets for the consideration of full retirement age[iv] and without any changes to the system, Social Security is estimated to be insolvent by 2035[v]. Some of the best economist minds have been on the case for a while and have solutions that will result in solvency[vi]. However, these solutions will need to reach bipartisan political backing and would potentially lead to some short-term financial pain. Ultimately, we do not believe that Social Security will disappear in 2035 but we do help people consider and prepare for the possibility that it may look a little different than the current projections.

Many firefighters, police officers, teachers, and other public sector workers are still set to receive pensions in the future. But the reality of the situation is that we saw many of those pension benefits reduced in the early 2010s and most employers do not offer pension programs to their employees. The number of people in the United States with a pension has gone down by nearly half from 1980 to 2008[vii]. Even since 2008, we have seen dozens of large companies performing pension buyouts to get the obligation off their books.

We know a lot of people who are exasperated by the perceived lack of consistency and reliability of pensions and Social Security. The people we have spoken with say things like, "This thing has been mismanaged," and "I have very little faith that it will pay out." The truth is that actuarial calculations are not perfect and there are a lot of moving parts involved.

Pensions are a delicate balance between managing investment returns, guessing at population growth, and guessing when people are going to die.

For the most part, Social Security and other pensions operate by having those currently working help fund those currently retired. Ideally, we would have a steadily growing population where there are always more people working than people retired. However, population growth is not linear. Birth rates are dropping. Generation X has a smaller population than the Baby Boomers and Generation Z has fewer people than Millennials[viii]. We cannot simply depend on the next generation to fund this generation's retirement.

So, that is where we are today. It is largely our own responsibility to ensure our financial security in retirement. Because the basics of investing, compounding interest, budgeting, and taxation were not widely taught in school, this can be a scary prospect for many people. In the introduction, we gave the example of Cicely's friend, Cody, who took his idea of "a good income" of $200,000 and multiplied it by 50 years to end up with a retirement goal of $10 million.

Cody was going through a very basic version of the thought process of the actuaries who determine pension designs. He was guessing at how long he thought he would live and trying to stretch his money based on that. However, the idea of moving to cash and evenly dividing payments over your lifetime neglects a very important factor: inflation.

According to Ibbotson, average inflation is just around 3%, compounding over the last 100 years[ix]. If we assume about average inflation, that means that if Cody is 30 and plans to retire at 50, the cost of living will be about 1.81 times what it is now at age 50. He would have to have $361,222 to live the same lifestyle that $200,000 would afford today. By the time he is age 80, the cost of living would be nearly 4.4 times what it is when he was 30. That annual dollar amount would be $876,781. The moral of the story is that if you are not gaining more than inflation on average for retirement assets, you are losing significant purchasing power every year.

Imagining Your Retirement

Those thinking about retirement should also consider what kind of lifestyle they want to live. If you are currently living in a major metropolitan city with a high cost of living – like San Francisco, Los Angeles, Portland, Seattle, New York City, Miami, Denver, or Austin – but dream of living a more rural life, you may want to re-assess your cost of living. You also want to think about the income taxes in your state versus the state or country you may end up in.

In budgeting, we want to consider at what age we want to achieve financial independence, where we want to retire, if and how much we want to travel, if we want to take on new expensive hobbies, our family history of longevity/illness, whether or not we may become financially responsible for a sibling or parent, whether we will still have debt obligations to pay off like a mortgage, and if we want to continue part-time work. That is on an individual level. But if you are in a partnership, retirement is a team sport.

Every couple is different, and it is important to communicate early and often about the goals on both sides. We find so often that in a given couple, one person may want to stop working and pursue a passion project as early as financially possible, whereas the other person may picture themselves working well into their 70s or even 80s because that is what the rest of their family did.

Generally, we recommend coming up with a "nice to have" number and a "we can live on this" number in today's dollars. Then, we can apply inflation, taxes, and investment returns in the different phases of life. As we said, we do not believe in a magic number for retirement. Things change in life. Longevity, interest rates, volatility, inflation, and taxes are variable and can be unpredictable. We recommend doing the best we can with the information we have and regularly assessing our progress toward our financial goals.

Once people have their savings goals in mind, one of the most common questions we get from our clients is on the matter of taxes. As an employee of an organization, you may have a pre-tax or Roth savings option in a retirement plan. The reason that people save in retirement programs is because of the tax-advantaged nature.

Traditional Taxation

In a pre-tax plan, every dollar saved today is a deduction that reduces what you pay in taxes today. You get a bigger bang for your buck on what you are saving. Those dollars saved are invested and as the money grows, you do not owe taxes on that growth. Not paying taxes on growth of assets leads to compounding interest. When you do end up pulling money from your retirement account, you pay taxes based on your future income tax bracket.

Roth Taxation

In a Roth plan, every dollar saved today is after taxes. It feels just like if you saved in a bank account or other brokerage account. However, as the money grows and as you distribute it, you are not paying taxes ever again if you withdraw after the age of 59 ½. This predictable nature of the Roth taxation is why we save a significant portion of our retirement savings in the Roth sleeve. Because of this, some will say Roth-style taxation is the best way to save. However, we do not deal in absolutes and so-called magic solutions.

It is true that today's marginal tax rates are historically low. For those concerned about tax rates in the future, Roth savings can reduce the risk of taxation above expectations. However, we recommend consulting your tax professional based on your goals and current tax situation. If we do not expect to need nearly as much income as we are earning today, pre-tax investments and getting current deductions might serve us well.

We find many in their early income-earning years to prefer Roth taxation because their income and cost of living may be the lowest in their lives. In peak income-earning years, we find that people are more likely to opt for pre-tax to minimize today's costs and may expect to need less in retirement.

Lesson in Compounding Interest

Regardless of whether you save your money pre-tax or Roth, you are getting the benefit of compounding interest. The nice thing about compounding interest is that the earlier you start saving, the less you must save over your life. You may have taken a math class sometime in your life where they mentioned the "Rule of 72." The basic premise of the rule is that you take the number 72 and divide it by the compounding returns you are getting and that is the amount of time your money takes to double. Here is some easy math: let's say hypothetically that you are getting 7.2% returns; 72 divided by 7.2% is 10. It will take 10 years to double your money.

So often, we find that our younger clients are both more concerned for retirement and on better track for it than some of those who come to us closer to retirement. With time and compounding interest, a little bit can go a long way. Often, the contribution recommendation given expected budget, retirement age, taxes, and inflation are not fully to the maximum one can save. For those financially able or who need the tax savings, we generally think it is prudent to maximize what you can save in an employer-sponsored plan.

In short, there is no silver bullet or magic number in retirement planning. It is our responsibility to plan the best we can based on our needs, understanding that things can change. We know this is a lot to consider, but we hope that you take away that retirement planning does not have to be this scary thing looming over you – if you start making small steps today. If you need guidance for going through this thought process or seeing how you are progressing, we recommend speaking with a financial professional.

CHAPTER 3:
College Planning

CICELY'S GRANDFATHER has always told her that when he went to college in California, he was able to pay the $2,000 per semester expense with his part-time job. Since then, things have gone through a few changes.

In the 21st century alone, the cost of college has more than doubled, with an annualized cost increase of 6.8% per year to a whopping $35,331 per year on average as of 2022[x]. We are also finding that, unlike in the times of our grandparents, taking on a job or even two in college is usually not enough to support those rising costs. Student loan debt is the single largest form of personal debt in the nation, topping out at $1.75 trillion[xi].

Because of all of this, parents of teenagers, parents of young children, and couples who are thinking about maybe someday having children all come to us with questions about how the heck they will be able to send their child to college. It is a serious concern, and the most basic answer is that they can send their child to get an undergraduate degree under a lot of different scenarios:

1. Parents/grandparents save 100% of college cost and give child full ride from investment.
2. Parents/grandparents save some of college costs and supplement the rest with income from working.
3. Parents/grandparents entirely pay for college costs from their income.
4. Parents/grandparents save some of college cost, child gets a job and takes loans for the rest.

5. Parents/grandparents pay for some of college from income, child gets job and takes loans for the rest.
6. Parents/grandparents save some of college cost, child earns scholarship for the remainder.
7. Child earns full ride scholarship
8. Child gets job and takes loans for the entirety of college cost

This does not even consider some scenarios that would remove funding considerations for college from the picture. Here are some examples:

1. Child joins the military.
2. Child pursues trade school.
3. Child pursues life as an "influencer."
4. Child decides to live abroad.

Okay, that third one was sort of a joke, but we're sure you catch our drift. Just like in retirement planning, there are a lot of considerations when thinking about college planning. We do not hold any judgements for any ways that our friends and clients think about this issue. No matter what that looks like, we do encourage figuring out which situation you are in early.

For young children and those not born yet, it can be tough to figure out their direction or what you see for them. We have seen lots of parents guess at some aspects while their children are young.

We have clients we'll call Krista and Brian, who both went to university on athletic scholarships and see an early propensity in their children for gifts in athletics. As of now, we are planning for somewhere between scenario 5 and 6. Just like with retirement planning, these plans can change as goals adjust. If their son, Jimmy, decides at 15 that he wants to quit baseball to spend more time in drama, then we would want to reassess this plan.

High Achievers from High Earning Families

There is also a lot that families can do to prepare for this potential cost, especially with students who are academically inclined, very involved in extracurriculars, and/or doing well in sports.

Many families assume that if they will not qualify for need-based aid, that they will need to pay for college in its entirety. Families may not qualify for need-based aid if they have joint household income greater than about $200,000. Let's say a family had two back-to-back kids and have a household income of $250,000. If those kids were both college-age today and the parents opt to cover this from income, that would add a whopping $70,662 in annual expenses on average. Many families, even in the more affluent segments, would have a hard time adding over $70,000 to their annual expenses.

The good news is that need-based aid is not the only option for children looking to get some of college paid for. For children that show an early drive and desire to go to college, merit scholarships, or scholarships based on achievement, can lessen the financial burden as well.

Our employer has long offered scholarships to high school seniors. So occasionally, we would go to scholarship nights at high schools to present the scholarships and see the number of companies also offering merit scholarships to the seniors. We also noticed that there were very few high school seniors who applied for these scholarships, with the same 10 receiving the large bulk of scholarships because they were the ones who applied for the scholarships. A friend of Cicely's was able to pay for half of her private university education from merit scholarships, even though her family was considered high income because she did her research and applied.

Thinking about merit scholarships and achievements early can improve the outcomes of the schools the children get into. It also gives these young adults some skin in the game of their education without having them take on massive loans.

Even with merit scholarships, parents may want to have a little bit saved for things like housing and food if they do want to avoid taking on loans. There is also the potential that the student does not want to put the hours of work into researching and applying for scholarships and college, so it must be funded another way. We will discuss other ways to cover college expenses at the end of this section.

High Achievers from Families that are Not High Income

Between need-based financial aid and merit scholarships, taking the time and putting in the work to apply for these scholarships can often pay for a significant chunk of expense at most schools. A word of caution is that some of the offerings we speak about for college savings count against Free Application for Federal Student Aid (FAFSA). If it is likely that a student will qualify for need-based financial aid, that would be a factor to consider.

Good Students from High Earning Families

We consider a good student to be someone who takes some, but not all, advanced placement classes and gets As, Bs, and maybe even a C or two in school. They may also be part of a club or sport, but they are not high achieving in the organizations. This type of student may not qualify for need-based aid and may be unlikely to apply for merit scholarships.

This student may consider community college for a couple years before transferring to a four-year university or might go straight to a cheaper public university. For this, we would be looking at saving in advance, paying from income, or having the student take on loans.

Good Students from Families that are Not High Income

The potential to qualify for need-based aid certainly goes up for a good student not coming from a high-earning family, but there is a good chance that the need-based aid would not cover the entire cost of a four-year university. If a student is very decisive and knows what they want to do for a living, going straight to a university might make sense for them to take on the loans and/or get a job.

If a student is still figuring it out, community college before a four-year comes at a much lower cost and can lessen the burden of the potential loans. Many communities offer very low or even free tuition to community colleges.

Those Who Are Not Academically Inclined

For some, going to a four-year university is simply not a good fit. If a high school student and the family alike know that, then college planning is relatively simple. There were plenty of individuals from Cicely's hometown who did not pursue a college degree out of high school and went on to lead successful lives in a wide range of careers, including sales, metal working, carpentry, and the military.

Vehicles to Save for College

We will discuss how to think about investing and asset allocation in another section. Here, we discuss asset location, or the vehicle we choose to invest in. When considering a college savings vehicle, one of the most important considerations is time horizon. Just like with retirement savings, the earlier we start saving for college, the less we generally must save overall and the more tax advantages we can get.

If parents start planning for college at the birth of their child, then they have an 18-year investment time horizon before they need to start withdrawing funds. If a family started saving $400 per month and received a hypothetical 8% compounding interest* for 18 years, they will have saved $86,400 and have $179,761.17 to spend on college.

However, not every investment vehicle allows for compounding interest. When we have a long investment time horizon and a high tolerance for risk, it may make sense to look at a tax-advantaged vehicle for college funding.

*NOTE: this hypothetical example is not indicative of the actual performance of any particular investment, insurance contract, or other financial product, nor does it account for the impact of any fees or taxes.

In the last chapter, we discussed pre-tax and Roth taxation. If a parent will be over the age of 59 ½ when their child is in college, then they can use tax-advantaged retirement funds to fund college. We want to emphasize that we would generally only recommend considering this if you reviewed your financial plan and found that you were over-funded for your retirement budget needs by more than the annual cost of college for four years. We can take loans for education funding, but nobody will give you a loan for retirement funding.

When thinking about college funding, many people may have heard of a Section 529 college savings plan (also referred to as a 529). While incomparable to a Roth IRA in fundamental ways, 529 college savings plans have similar taxation to a Roth account. Unlike with a Roth IRA, families can save up to their own gift tax exclusion ($17,000 per person in 2023) or front-load five years of savings into the vehicle ($85,000 per person in 2023).

To recap Roth taxation, after-tax money goes in, it grows tax-deferred, and it is taken out tax-free when used for the purpose it is intended for. The purpose of a 529 is covering qualified education expenses, including things like tuition, books, room/board (on campus), and some transportation costs. A limited amount may be converted into a Roth IRA for the child if they cannot be used for qualified higher education expenses as of 2023.

Cicely went to University of California, Santa Barbara for school and many students choose not to live on campus after their first year. If she'd had a 529, she would have been penalized if she used the account for most of her housing costs. The penalty is 10% on any growth in the 529 above what you put in, in addition to state and federal income taxes on the gains in the 529 college savings account.

In the earlier hypothetical example, the cost basis was $86,400 and the funds were valued at $179,761.17. If you took the amount in full for non-qualified expenses, the tax penalty would be about $9,336, plus income taxes. If those income taxes were 24%, we would be losing 34% of our total gains, which is higher than long term capital gains on a taxable investment in 2023.

The 529 also is the account that counts against FAFSA and makes it difficult to qualify for need-based financial aid.

A Coverdell Education Savings Account is an account very similar to the 529. This type of vehicle receives the same tax treatment as a 529 but has limited funding ability. This can be a viable option for those in a lower income bracket who just want to set aside some funds for higher education purposes. In 2023 annual contributions were limited to $2,000 per year, making it difficult to accumulate at the level a 529 can. It also comes with the same limitations regarding tax penalties and FAFSA qualification.

A vehicle some parents consider is known as a Uniform Transfers to Minors Account (UTMA) or Uniform Gifts to Minors Account (UGMA). For simplicity, we will only discuss UTMA, since this is the more poplar of the two. Family members still have the $17,000 gifting ability within an investment account in the name of the minor child that is being invested. This account does not have any special tax deferment or advantages of the other vehicles we discussed.

The main advantage of a UTMA account comes when the guardian of the account has a significant income and would be subject to much more taxation on the account's gains than the minor child. The first portion of gains are instead taxed at the minor child's bracket, potentially saving money on annual taxation. If there is significant investment income, there is a portion that still gets taxed at the parent's bracket. Many shy away from this kind of investment because once the child reaches adulthood (18-years-old in most states), the funds are placed in the child's name, and they have full access for any purpose. Some hesitate to give their children full decision-making and budget-management authority. Since this account becomes the asset of the child, it also counts against FAFSA, and they would be unlikely to get financial aid if a significant amount has been saved.

Many families we talk to have grown up watching TV commercials where cash value life insurance is mentioned as a college funding vehicle. Unlike the Roth IRA, 529 plans, and Coverdell, the primary purpose of life insurance is death benefit protection. The cash value, which is a combination of premiums paid and investment returns, of a permanent life insurance policy may be accessed for any reason without taxation on the growth. However, life insurance only receives the tax benefits if it remains in force for one's entire life. Loans and withdrawals also reduce the permanent life insurance policy's cash value and death benefit and increase the chance that the policy may lapse. If the policy lapses, matures, is surrendered, or falls out of IRS compliance, the loan balance at such time would generally be viewed as distributed and taxable under the general rules for distributions of life insurance policy cash values.

We will address life insurance in more depth in a future chapter but remember that it is designed for longer time horizons and, first and foremost, to provide death benefit protection for designated beneficiaries. Life insurance is not considered in FAFSA, so a student may still be able to qualify for need-based aid if their parent has a life insurance policy.

Lastly, there are plenty of ways one may save outside of a tax-advantaged vehicle, particularly if we are starting to save closer to the time that a student goes to college. One can save in a brokerage account in accordance with their risk tolerance and time horizon or even in cash if the student is close to college age. Investments within the brokerage account would be subject to investment risk, including the potential loss of principal. Gains in a brokerage account would be subject to capital gains taxation upon sale of the investments, so there is a little more thought that needs to go into tax management and figuring the net amount needed for college.

CHAPTER 4:

Major Purchase Planning

MANY CHILDREN GROW UP desiring the American Dream. You know what we're talking about: the perfect spouse, the perfect white picket fence home, and the perfect 2.5 children. Many people dream of buying a home, but major purchases can be a house, a boat, a business, or anything in between.

Before starting on how to plan for a major purchase, we want to emphasize that it is okay to rent forever. We have come across so many couples that are house poor, meaning that they are spending so much on their mortgage, property taxes, homeowner's insurance, and routine maintenance that they cannot really afford to do other things. Because of this phenomenon, many couples who do own homes have the vast majority (sometimes even all) of their assets in their home.

It's Okay to Rent Forever

Cicely was having a conversation with a friend recently and she said, "I feel like I need to buy a house, but I really like the rent-controlled apartment I am renting." Cicely dug a little deeper to find that this friend really did not have an emotional connection to purchasing a home but rather saw it as an investment opportunity. She thought the price of the house would appreciate so much over time that she could eventually sell it for a lot of profit.

Her thought process comes from the fact that the last 10 years have been some of the highest for national housing prices, with an average annualized rate of return of 7.6% as of September 2022, according to the S&P Shiller-

Case Housing Index[xii]. For comparison, the average for the S&P 500 large cap stock index has been 11.88% since adopting the 500 stocks to the index in 1957[xiii]. Robert Shiller, one of the economists involved in the Shiller-Case Index, found that most periods of time in housing are not like the last 10 years. Housing has kept pace with inflation for over 50-year periods, including 1890-1946[xiv]. Keep in mind that there are fundamental differences between investing in real estate and investing in the stock market, each with its own inherent risks, time horizons, costs, and other factors – and neither is suitable for all investors.

Some people will make an argument that they can gain leverage when buying a home, making it an even better investment. Someone might be in a favorable position if they assume house prices will increase and if they could get a 0% down, low interest rate loan. However, many couples we see rush to pay their houses off and put significant down payments on homes, often due to negative feelings about carrying debt. Pure price appreciation of real estate is certainly not the only factor that determines whether real estate would be a good investment. We simply wanted to present this data because many of our own clients struggle to scrape up the cash to buy a first home or investment property because they have learned from their upbringing that real estate investing is "the only way to become rich." We are here to tell you it is not the only way, by a long shot.

The potential for price appreciation in residential real estate also does not necessarily account for the fact that homes come with costs outside of the mortgage payment and interest. According to a 2021 Bankrate study, 64% of millennials have regrets about their home purchases and one of the biggest regrets was ongoing costs[xv]. Homeowners must pay property taxes, get homeowner's insurance, and plan for unexpected maintenance. Renters, for the most part, do not have significant surprise costs above and beyond rent. If the toilet breaks, renters call the landlord. If there's mold, renters call the landlord. Homeowners do not have the luxury of passing maintenance costs on to someone else.

So, if the draw is not emotional and the potential buyer is looking at a purchase from a pure price appreciation standpoint, renting versus buying deserves thoughtful consideration.

Considerations in Budgeting for a New Home

We work in the San Francisco Bay Area, and here, houses come at an exorbitant cost. For people to live in a neighborhood they may want to live in, even with a significant down payment, mortgage costs alone could easily be in the five figures. If you are in a two-income household making $250,000 per year and have a $10,000 monthly mortgage, the mortgage alone could be close to 70% of net monthly income depending on the state and taxes at the time.

As we mentioned in the prior section, it is important to consider all the expenses that go into owning a home prior to purchasing. Just like with everything in financial planning, it is important to think about goals, first and foremost. If this is going to be a couple's primary residence, we recommend quickly figuring out the non-financial non-negotiables. Here are examples of some of these considerations: town/city, neighborhood, school districts, proximity to work, proximity to parks, local restaurants, and house size. Once we have that figured out, we can estimate what that cost would be today.

From a capital appreciation and leverage standpoint, getting a down payment as close to zero as possible could make sense. But many couples aim to put 20% down on a home to avoid having to pay for mortgage insurance. Mortgage insurance is basically an insurance policy to protect the bank if your home value goes down and you end up underwater on the loan. It is important to remember that leverage works in both directions. If you have $60,000 in equity in a $300,000 home and the value goes down to $220,000, your equity is -$20,000. In 2008, many people defaulted on their mortgages when they got into this situation.

If a couple goes through all their home-buying goals and finds that a home meeting all their non-financial goals costs $500,000 and they do not want to be responsible for coming up with mortgage insurance, then they would want to come up with that 20% down payment of $100,000. However, that is not the only consideration. We urge couples to take a hard look at their budget.

If the mortgage alone is going to be significantly more than monthly rental expenses and the couple is generally not saving a lot each month, couples will want to consider reviewing their monthly budget and practice living on the adjusted expenses while they are saving for the home. Let's say a couple makes $175,000 jointly (let's call it $122,500 after taxes). In that scenario, their after-tax discretionary income would be $10,208 per month. If they are spending about $10,000 per month, the breakdown might be something like $3,000 to rent, $1,000 to car payments and insurance, $2,000 to groceries and eating out, $2,000 per month to childcare/pet care expenses, and an additional $2,000 buffer for vacations and weekend trips.

Let's say that the couple in this example inherited some money or sold some company stock to pay for the down payment and the home that they are looking to purchase will have a $6,000 mortgage payment. Monthly taxes and fees may add an additional $1,340 depending on the state (property taxes and insurance requirements vary by state and area). The couple's monthly mandatory housing outlay is going from $3,000 to $7,340. Basically, for a couple with this budget, it would mean eliminating vacations/weekend trips and reducing their food budget significantly.

If we are going to end up house poor with a home purchase meeting our criteria, then it may not be the time to purchase. If a couple's room in their budget is $3,000 per month for a home, we would say that they should consider building up the down payment for more time, so they do not have to borrow as much, take a harder look at their non-negotiables, and consider purchasing a more inexpensive home.

This line of reasoning often leads to people seeking to purchase condos. A condo may be less expensive than a stand-alone home, depending on what you're looking for. But they have some key trade-offs to be aware of. First off, usually condo owners must pay a homeowner's association fee. Usually, this fee is subject to being raised. We've had many clients end up selling their condos because their homeowner's association fees became too exorbitant to fit into their budget. Another potential pitfall to be aware of is that not all the maintenance expenses would be within your control.

For example, Cicely lived in a condo where the plumbing in the kitchen got backed up to the point of flooding the kitchen with water mixed with everything people poured down the drains. She called a plumber who promptly told her that he sees this sort of thing all the time with shared piping in condos. It was likely some people in the building were pouring things down the sink that they should not have, such as oils and coffee grounds. Because of this, the tenants of the building had to negotiate major work on the pipes to prevent the backup from rearing its ugly head again.

Once a couple has decided on the home price, saved for the down payment, and worked the monthly payments comfortably into their budget, they should also consider having a bit of an extra buffer for unexpected expenses. Purchasing a home comes with significant closing costs, inspection costs, potential furniture purchases, and potential repairs needed that were not considered in the initial decision process.

For most couples, we want to have three-to-six months of monthly expenses in cash in the bank. For those purchasing a home, we'd lean closer to that six-month number. In our example couple with $10,000 monthly expenses, they would want to have $60,000 above and beyond the down payment amount they are seeking.

We will discuss investing and considerations for growing money towards this goal in the investing section of this book.

Acquiring a House

In the budgeting section, we reviewed some things to consider when thinking about how to acquire a house. The biggest consideration is the purpose and motivations behind the purchase. Are we hoping to appreciate the value significantly over time? Are we buying for purely emotional reasons? Are we hoping to get a cash flow from the property?

Each person in a couple may have different motivations for the purchase. Once you figure out your motivations, we would recommend bringing in an expert to consult, unless you happen to be an expert yourself. Just like consulting a doctor for your medical questions and a financial advisor for getting toward your financial goals, it helps to work with an experienced realtor who specializes in the type of property and area you are seeking. Once in place, they may be able to introduce you to off-market listings, negotiate on your behalf, and generally answer questions about the buying process.

Other Types of Major Purchases

We come across many clients who have various other major purchase goals. One said he'd like to fund a sailing adventure for his whole family for two years. We've had many say that they'd like to leave the corporate world someday and start their own business. For any major purchase, it's important to identify our priorities. Start off by figuring out emotionally what you would like. Do you love books and want to open a bookstore someday? Do you love building things and want to start a construction company? Have you worked yourself to the bone and just want to plan a year-long vacation?

Once we have identified our goals, then it's time to figure out when we would like to achieve them. When we pose this question to clients, the answer often depends on how satisfied they are with the status quo. When people have a very stressful job and they are thinking about starting their own business, they will often say as soon as possible. Whether you are in a hurry or not, there's much to consider when making major purchase goals.

Starting A Business

Cicely's parents grew up with a dream to never have a boss. As she was growing up, she got to see that dream come true for them. Anyone who has ever had a business idea probably has gotten very excited about the prospect of solving a problem. There is a lot of capital and time required from the inception of an idea to running a successful business with a positive cash flow.

When considering starting a business, it is important to know the source of funding. Here are some examples of how people fund new ventures:

- Bootstrapping
- Friends and Family Money
- Business Loans
- Angel Investors
- Venture Capital

Often, there will be a combination of a few of these methods. It is also important to research similar businesses and speak with the owners about how they were able to build the business and some of the costs associated. Those costs can include space, equipment, compliance, accounting, marketing, formation, and many more. By speaking with people who have been in that position, you may avoid serious pitfalls and budget appropriately. As with the home purchase, we recommend keeping excess cash and not overstretching one's budget. A home should not be someone's only asset and neither should a business.

Buying a Business

When buying a business, the same major purchase principles we already discussed apply. Buying a business would usually be funded through cash or bank loans. When seeking to buy a business, using a business broker or other trusted professional is generally advisable. A business broker will decide on a fair value for the business and facilitate the transaction and agreements.

Funding a Vacation or Trip

For this type of major purchase, you would want to plan for all conceivable expenses and leave some extra room in that budget. A vacation or trip should be funded entirely from cash or liquid cash alternatives.

PART 2:
Investment Management

CHAPTER 5:

Introduction to Investment Management

WHILE WE CAN THINK of the goals-based objectives described in part one as the destination, we can then think of the investment management piece of the financial puzzle as both the vehicle for and the road toward that destination.

It could be relatively easy to decide how to invest. But given the array of products, services, and approaches available in the investing world today, the average young couple may become confused and end up doing nothing

Here is a traveling example: if you know you want to go from San Francisco to Seattle, you have a multitude of options for how to get there. For example, let's say you plan on driving. Not only do you have to decide what route to take if you are going to drive (scenic route? fastest route? tolls? no tolls?) but you also must decide if you're going to drive your own car, rent a car, which company you will rent from, etc. If you're going to fly, you have another host of options: airlines, time, price, economy vs. first class, etc. Or maybe you want to take a train, choosing between a sleeper car and coach. We may not necessarily recommend this option, but you could even hitchhike.

We are reminded of a conversation we had with a young couple. When asked what they wanted their money to do for them, they said they wanted to invest in ETFs. ETF stands for exchange traded fund, of which there are literally thousands with different investment objectives. It basically just means basket of stocks that trade on an exchange. Saying you want to invest in ETFs as your financial goals is like asking a traveler where she wants to go and having her say, "I want to go on a plane." That plane, of course, could take you almost anywhere.

CHAPTER 6:

Our Investment Philosophy at Its Most Basic

IN THIS PART, we lay out our basic investment management philosophy and how that philosophy then leads into investment strategy. There are essentially two opposing philosophies on how to invest:

1) Investing as if you have foresight and believe strongly in what may happen in the future.
2) Investing as if you don't have foresight and do not have any idea of what may happen in the future.

Depending on which philosophy you hold, you will have very different investing strategies.

With the first philosophy, if you believe that you know what may happen in securities markets, you might own individual stocks and other securities. You might even be highly leveraged (borrowing money to fund your positions), short (speculating against securities with unlimited downside to your positions), and concentrate your portfolio in just a few names, regardless of your personal risk tolerance.

As you can imagine, this strategy has the potential to reap even substantial gains if you are correct. If you are wrong, however, the consequences could be severely negative with the potential for substantial losses, mainly because past market performance is never a guarantee or even reliable indication of future results. It is not possible to predict or perfectly truly time investment market outcomes.

With the second philosophy, you will own broad market positions, avoid shorting and leverage, practice broad international diversification, and allocate based on your risk tolerance.

With this, your ride to your objective won't be nearly as exciting as the first, but it has the potential to be much smoother and you'll have an enhanced potential for achieving your financial goals

When it comes to implementing an investment strategy, one of the fundamental principles of any sound investment plan is to match the asset allocation to the risk tolerance. The greater the risk tolerance, the more risk exposure may be appropriate and suitable for the asset allocation.

Asset allocation is the percentage of a portfolio in different asset classes, such as stocks, bonds, real estate, cash, etc. Risk tolerance is the ability and willingness to withstand volatility, or asset price movement – both up and down – in the portfolio.

If the risk tolerance is high, one might consider being more heavily invested in stocks and other risky asset classes. If the risk tolerance is low, a portfolio might be better weighted more towards bonds, cash, and other less risky asset classes.[xvi]

Let's take two contrasting hypothetical examples: a 22-year-old recent college graduate investing his money in a Roth IRA and a 74-year-old retired widow who needs income from her portfolio to meet ongoing expenses.

The recent college graduate investing money in his Roth IRA may have a very high risk tolerance for several reasons. The primary reason is the long investment timeframe. A Roth IRA cannot be accessed without taxes and penalties on the gains until age 59.5, so he has more than 37 years to invest and to ride out any stock downturns during that period. The second reason is that with a Roth IRA, unlike a traditional IRA, taxes are paid upfront and then the gains are never taxed. Because of this, investing more aggressively and taking on more risk for the potential to achieve higher gains over time in a Roth IRA – rather than in a traditional retirement account where gains are taxed at withdrawal – could make sense for this investor. The third reason is that the 22-year-old has many years of income that can help offset any investment losses during his working years.

On the other hand, the 74-year-old retired widow who needs income from her portfolio to meet ongoing expenses has a very low risk tolerance, and therefore should consider investing accordingly. For example, if she had invested 100% of her portfolio in high-risk stocks in 2008, she would have likely sustained substantial losses that year. If she had been withdrawing at that time to receive consistent income, she probably would have had to cut her living expenses back sharply, assuming she didn't want to cut into any of her principal.

We use these two individuals as examples to show contrast to make a point. Most people, and especially our young couple clients, fall somewhere in between. Overall, it's important to remember that investing involves risk, including loss of principal invested, and that each investor should carefully consider his or her own unique set of circumstances, needs, goals, time horizon, tolerance for risk, and what's appropriate and suitable for them in determining when and how to invest.

There are other considerations when it comes to risk tolerance, including the source of wealth (was it achieved actively, through investing or an entrepreneurial business? Or was it achieved passively, such as through inheritance or many years of working at a larger organization?), and measure of wealth (how much the client "feels" they have).

Overall, many considerations go into determining risk tolerance, but matching risk tolerance to asset allocation is one of the fundamental components of financial planning.

CHAPTER 7:

Your Investment Options: Active, Passive, or Evidence Based?

ONCE YOU SET YOUR GOALS, you will have a myriad of options of how to implement an investment strategy. If you decide to work with a financial advisor, you may find that they have two broad ways they could help you as you implement your strategy (depending on the type of firm they represent, their specific registrations and licensing, and the type of services and products they offer).

They'll probably say:

1. They can do it entirely or partially on your behalf by creating their own allocations, taking views on individual stocks or individual markets/sectors/geographies, and choosing mutual funds, or exchange traded funds for you.
2. They can offer what are called "centrally managed platforms." In these types of platforms, much of the investment management decisions and actions – the trading, stock and fund selection, rebalancing, market timing is all done by a third-party investment manager.

With the second option, there are still a host of options that you must decide on in working with your financial advisor, as there are hundreds of fund companies, and thousands of combinations of different funds.

Out of all centrally managed platforms, we've narrowed the multitude of options down to three general categories: active, passive, and evidence based.

Active Management

Active management is the concept of choosing individual stocks, sectors, industries, or even geographies to generate return potential for a client's portfolio, or for a fund (or pooled client accounts) that will seek to beat a benchmark.

Active management dates back to the 1920s when mutual funds were first established.

Passive Management

Another option would be passive investment management, or just tracking indexes. For example, many funds that invest in large company US stocks try to beat the S&P 500 – the 500 largest companies in the US by market capitalization (number of shares outstanding multiplied by price per share) each year. Other indices include the Russell 2000, a small company index, and the NASDAQ, an index of technology stocks.

Passive management originated in the early 1970s, when Vanguard founder Jack Bogle started the first index fund that tracked the S&P 500.

Moreover, from a fee perspective, the companies that make primarily index funds tend to have comparatively lower fees. This is, in part, because these funds do not have to pay research analysts to do fundamental stock analysis. They also have much lower marketing and distributions costs.

Finally, from a tax perspective, index funds tend to have lower tax drag than other funds, in part due to lower turnover ratios. Index funds are not buying and selling as frequently – in fact, they are often only buying and selling once or twice a year when the index is reconstituted. Therefore, they tend to generate lower capital gains than actively managed funds. Of course, note that index funds do still have tax drag as they generate capital gains when stocks exit the index and taxes on dividends as well. Keep in mind that it is not possible to invest directly in an index.

Evidence Based Management

There is a third, and much lesser well-known, approach to investment management called "Evidence Based Investing." The idea with evidence-based investing is to move beyond passive management, with an approach grounded in financial science.

It was founded in 1981 when Eugene Fama of the University of Chicago and David Booth decided to start Dimensional Fund Advisors (DFA). Fama would go on to win the Nobel Prize in Economics in 2013, and Booth is the namesake of the University of Chicago MBA program after donating $300 million gift in 2008.

Evidence-based investing is an approach to building portfolios in the stock and bond markets that seeks to outperform the market indexes.

The approach involves something called a "premium." (These premiums are also referred to as "factors" or "dimensions.") Premiums are essentially potential advantages in returns that certain segments of the market, or characteristics of stocks, have.

For example, in the stock market, there is a small cap premium, where smaller companies' stocks may outperform larger companies' stocks. There is also a value premium, where companies that are cheaper may outperform more expensive companies. There's even a profitability premium, where more profitable companies may outperform less profitable companies.

In short, there are three general types of centrally managed platforms: 1) Active funds that seek to beat a benchmark using forecasting and research, 2) passive funds that track indexes, and 3) evidence-based funds that use the "premiums" in their approach. Every investor needs to decide what, if any, approach may be appropriate for them. Overall, investing involves risk, including loss of principal invested.

CHAPTER 8:

Emotions in Investing and Methods to Handle Them

"THE EPIPHANY I had in my career in randomness came when I understood that I was not intelligent enough, nor strong enough, to even try to fight my emotions." – Nassim Nicholas Taleb in *Fooled by Randomness*

One of the most difficult aspects of following a financial plan that includes a stock or public security component is the ability to stick with the plan when emotions will tell you otherwise.

The most classic example is that when stocks are going down in price, it can be very painful emotionally. It is true for everyone, no matter how long they have been investing.

Dan is reminded of a panel he put together that a gentleman named Jerry Dodson, who founded Parnassus Investments in 1984, was on. An audience member asked Jerry, who had been investing for over 30 years, if he still felt negative emotions after buying a stock that then proceeded to go further down. Jerry said that of course he still felt the emotion of loss. Emotional reactions to gains and losses are hardwired into our brains.

When Dan was a hedge fund manager, he would at first keep his positions on his screen at all times. He remembers feeling a "relief" at 1 pm PST when the market closed, since the movements up and down no longer affected his emotions. He eventually decided to only look at positions at the close of each day, and later decided to only look once a week. As you can imagine, looking once a week involved much less emotional turmoil.

At one point, Dan even held one position that made up over 5% of his portfolio when the company filed for bankruptcy. This caused him to run to the bathroom due to extreme nausea. Yes, these negative emotions from losing money can be so real they have physical side effects.

Nassim Nicholas Taleb, a veteran trader, in his book *Fooled by Randomness*, talks about traders who have lost significant amounts of money breaking their phones and screaming at their assistants.

Managing these emotions, and the potential actions that result from them, is critical to achieving success of the long-term plan. This point is particularly salient for young couples, who often have a large exposure to the stock market, given their long time horizons.

The best way to avoid the negative emotions that come from seeing mark to market losses in stocks is to limit exposure to regular movements of stock portfolios. Yes, consider turning off the news and remove the stock app from your phone (as Dan has).

In fact, Daniel Kahneman, the Nobel Prize-winning author of *Thinking, Fast and Slow*, (which Dan uses as the first text in the Behavioral Finance class that he teaches at the University of San Francisco) suggests that reviewing portfolio performance once a quarter is enough.

Furthermore, we might suggest that clients with long time horizons consider only looking at their portfolio during account reviews with their financial professionals. There are three reasons for this:

1) If performance has been negative and the client is negatively affected, the financial professional can coach the client through their emotions and remind them of the potential value of being in equities

in the first place, and how this is most compatible with their long-term goals.

2) Clients generally meet with their financial advisors only a few times a year. The longer the time horizon, the more potential for is that performance to be positive over the long term. Imagine if you checked only once every 10 years: 85% of the time since 1926 you would be happy, and only 15% sad.[xvii]

3) This is the appropriate time to discuss if the client would like to change an allocation. For example, maybe the client found out that their "willingness" – or emotional ability to withstand risk – is lower than they thought. Better to discuss this with a clear head than during an emotional swing due to a market dip. The client's goals might have changed as well. For example, they might have originally thought that all their money should go to retirement savings, but now might want to do a home purchase with some of those funds.

There is science behind this. Kahneman's "Prospect Theory" says that the pain of a loss will be greater than the equal pleasure of the same gain. So, in a $100 portfolio, for example, seeing your portfolio decline to $90 will be much more painful than the pleasure of watching it go to $110. [xviii]

You can imagine the ramifications of this. Small daily losses, mostly due to random noise in the market, will be emotionally draining, even if the daily wins and losses are of equal magnitude.

For Young Couples, Declines Can Actually Be Good News

We were recently doing an account review with a 29-year-old client, Joy, who was lamenting the fact that her retirement account had recently declined in value. Yes, as mentioned before, those negative emotions can be painful.

We pointed out to Joy that she had more than 30 years before she could even access those funds without penalties anyway, but she still told us it hurt.

While it's never fun to see account balances decline, it is a natural part of investing.

From a purely logical standpoint, a 29-year-old with a 30-year investing time horizon for retirement funds, market declines should be welcome.

After all, assuming that she contributes the maximum amount allowed into her qualified retirement plan, Joy will be investing an additional $600,000 (the 2022 contribution limit of $20,500 x 30) – and probably more as those limits go up – over the next 30 years. That pales in comparison to the amount she has already invested.

Future market declines will provide Joy the opportunity to buy in at even lower prices, raising her potential to profit over the long term from eventual gains. Anyone in the "accumulation phase" – or still building their wealth – should consider the potential value in market declines.

And for those in or closer to the "distribution phase" who need the money? Well, they should consider limiting their market exposure overall.

In short, if you're allocated to your risk tolerance – yes, you've heard us say it before – market movements over the long term may not necessarily impact the achievement of your long-term goals.

Limit News Intake

In addition to reframing declines as potentially positive over the long term, another way to avoid the negative emotions that come from portfolio fluctuations is to avoid or put into perspective most of the news, and certainly the financial news.

But research on this subject suggests that "very few of the aggregate price movements in the [equity] market show any meaningful association with headlines."[xix]

Another study, looking at the 50 largest equity market moves over 44 years, suggests that most of them did not actually correspond to *any* meaningful news.[xx]

In other words, major headlines can happen without causing large equity movements, and large equity movements can happen without any headlines at all.

We'll give you two more reasons:

The first is the excessive reporting of "noise over signal" in financial markets. Due to random movements (aka "noise"), on any given day some market will be up or down, and the media may find an explanation for it no matter how small the change. They will often have a story that includes an explanation for the move based on recent headlines.

One good example of this pattern comes from Nassim Nicholas Taleb's other book, *The Black Swan*, where he points out that the same headline – the capture of Iraqi dictator Saddam Hussein in December 2003 – was used to explain both a rise, and then fall, in U.S. Treasuries…the exact same day.

One only needs to look at everyday explanations of market activity to see examples of this. On the other hand, you might never see a headline that says, "The market declined by 0.05% today based on nothing but random noise." Humans seek causal explanations for all events – financial or otherwise – and the media is readily willing to provide them.

The second reason is what Nobel Laureate Robert Shiller has called "record overload." As Shiller writes, "If reporters look at the data enough in different ways, they will often find something that is close to setting a record on any given day."[xxi]

As your financial advisor, what would we suggest this means for you?

Read the news if you want. But consider whether the sensationalism with which financial news is presented should really have any impact on your portfolio or your investment decisions.

The basic principles of investing and portfolio allocation apply regardless of the headlines, and regardless of the uncertainty in the political or economic environments.

Talk to Your Financial Professional About How You Are Thinking and Feeling

If you choose to work with financial professionals, feel free to call them to set up a time to discuss how you are thinking and feeling about portfolio movements. Your advisor can guide you to discuss if you are on the right path or if that plan should be adjusted – and your risk tolerance or asset allocation changed - based on your psychological reactions to market movements.

According to Vanguard, half of the value of an advisor is "Behavioral Coaching" or "providing discipline and guidance" to clients. Vanguard even uses the term "emotional circuit breakers" to suggest that advisors can "circumvent clients' tendencies to chase returns or run for cover in emotionally charged markets."

Be Allocated to Risk Tolerance

While this section is not specifically about asset allocation*, we wanted to reemphasize its value as we do believe that being allocated according to your risk tolerance – both the ability to take on risk based on the facts of your financial situation, and the willingness to take on risk based on your psychological makeup – is also a strong factor in managing emotions.

For example, if that 29-year-old is invested with an aggressive risk tolerance, there is a reason for it and she can feel comfortable with her investing plan, even during market turmoil. A 55-year-old looking to retire in a few years has a lower risk tolerance and would therefore have less of their portfolio allocated to equity investments, which would be heavily impacted during market turmoil, and more allocated to fixed income investments, which tend to remain more stable during turmoil.

In short, if you're allocated to your risk tolerance, you have the greatest chance of achieving your financial goals. You'll also feel steadier along the way and able to manage the emotions that come with investing much easier.

* Asset allocation does guarantee a profit or protection against loss in a declining market.

CHAPTER 9:

Pitfalls to Avoid

WHEN NAVIGATING THE PATH towards your financial independence, there are many possible pitfalls to avoid, as tempting as they may sound.

Here are four:

1. Active Portfolio Management
2. Mimicking What Others Are Doing
3. Overreacting to Emotions
4. Overreacting to Events in the News

1. Active Portfolio Management

Being "active" with your investment portfolio can mean many things. It can mean picking your own stocks based on doing your own research. For workers at publicly traded companies, it can mean accumulating large positions in your company's stock. It can also mean attempting to time the overall market either yourself or putting your money with others who do.

We believe that all these approaches should be carefully considered. Think about whether active management in general should be avoided, based on your unique circumstances, goals, time horizon, and risk tolerance.

We strongly suggest that you carefully and thoughtfully consider the advisability of picking your own stocks for your portfolio before you do so. After all, if top professionals from top schools – those with the best resources and years of experience picking stocks – cannot necessarily beat the market, what chance does a novice have?

Another way to be "active" without even actively doing anything is to keep stock given to you by your employer. Over time, simply doing nothing can lead to a large portion of your portfolio being composed of stock in your own company. We suggest that you consider this carefully, as this is essentially active management. While you didn't buy the stock, it was just given to you, you are essentially picking it by holding on to it when there may be other options available to you to consider.

2. Mimicking What Others Are Doing

It can be very tempting to follow what others you know are doing. Many people like to brag about how much they made investing on their own, especially by buying individual stocks. Yet even if these stories are true, they will only tell you their winners, and rarely tell you about all the stocks they lost money on or their overall portfolio performance. This is called "confirmation bias" in the Behavioral Finance literature.

Confirmation bias is where "investors who believe they can pick winning stocks are regularly oblivious to their losing records, recording wins as evidence confirming their stock-picking skills but neglecting to record losses as disconfirming evidence."[xxii] More importantly, even if they did make money, that doesn't mean that their stock picking is necessarily part of a comprehensive financial plan. Finally, even if they are successful picking individual stocks, those same stocks may not be appropriate for you or your portfolio.

The best analogy we can give is this. Let's say you're at a cocktail party and someone tells you they've been taking a prescription drug that is making them feel great. They suggest that you, too, should take that drug. Would you do it? Unlikely. Because while it might be appropriate for them and their medical history, it may not be appropriate for you and your medical condition. Drugs should be prescribed by a medical professional, in the same way that an investing strategy should be informed by discussions with a qualified financial advisor to help determine if is appropriate for your financial circumstances and goals.

3. Reacting to Emotions

Emotions can be very powerful when it comes to investing – especially investing in stocks. Individual stocks and the overall market can widely fluctuate in price. Even large sections of the market can have big swings that can lead to painful negative emotions on down days or even down years. These emotions are very real and can sometimes be so bad they even have physical manifestations. No matter how long you have been investing, they still occur.

Research suggests that the pain of a loss in your portfolio is larger than the equivalent pleasure of a gain of equal size in your portfolio. This "Prospect Theory," as we mentioned earlier, is one reason why watching your stocks go up and down all day is emotionally painful. Experiencing the little losses – those red numbers on the screen – on a regular basis cause enough pain to offset the pleasure of an equal, or even higher, amount of gain.

While emotions are inescapable and we all will have them, it is important to make investment or economic decisions that aren't solely based on an emotional state. This "behavior coaching" is one of many areas where an advisor can be of assistance.

4. Reacting to Events in the News

It is easy to get sidetracked from your long-term investing goals by thinking that paying attention to the news media, and allocating your portfolio based on current events, is a wise way to make investment decisions.

Every day the news reports on violence or war in another country, climate change, headlines about what the Federal Reserve is doing or not doing, as well as other economic indicators. You may interpret a constant supply of reasons in the news to move your money around one way or the other, and this can be a constant temptation.

Yet studies that have looked at the news and market movement suggest that most news doesn't move the market and that most market movements are not reactions to news. In short, paying attention to the news media's views on where you should put your money, and then allocating accordingly, is not an advisable approach or strategy. As we've said many times, your investment strategy should be based on your individual goals and your risk tolerance, not your or anyone else's thoughts on where the market is going to go based on the news.

PART 3:
Risk Management

CHAPTER 10:

Introduction to Life Insurance

What is life insurance, and do you need it?

AT ITS MOST BASIC LEVEL, life insurance is a contract between you and the life insurance company where, in exchange for a payment from you called a "premium," the life insurance company agrees to pay a sum of money to your designated beneficiaries (called a "death benefit") in the event of your death. The higher the death benefit, the higher the premium.

Life insurance is an important consideration for most young couples because the greatest asset they have is their future earning power.

For example, take a two-earner couple, both age 30, each making $100,000 per year for a total of $200,000 combined. If this couple wanted to replace half of their income for their working careers from age 30 through age 65 – or $100,000 a year of income replacement, assuming a 3% increase every year of their salaries and discounting of their future earnings at 5% – this value is approximately $2.6 million. In other words, in the event of one of their deaths, to replace half of their future income between age 30 and 65, they would need $2.6 million today.

There are additional considerations in this type of insurance needs analysis. For example, the couple might want to secure additional funds beyond income replacement, possibly providing for college funding in the event of their death or paying off debts that might include a mortgage. They might also want to provide for additional funds for the first few years after loss, sometimes called "transitional income," and establish a level of emergency reserves.

Life insurance is not only for income earners. Indeed, a non-working spouse who takes care of young children might have life insurance because in the event of the non-working spouse's death the working spouse might need to hire a caregiver. A life insurance death benefit can provide this.

Given this background, there are several reasons to have life insurance for the death benefit alone:

1. If you have dependents who will rely on your future earnings
2. If you plan on having dependents who will rely on your future earnings
3. If you are a full or part time caregiver

There is an additional reason beyond the death benefit that it can make sense to have life insurance. This is because permanent life insurance – also referred to as cash value life insurance – will in value that can be accessed by the owner tax-free. Money that you've already paid taxes on is paid into the policy, that money grows tax-deferred, and then the owner can access it tax-free.

But keep in mind that the primary purpose of life insurance is to provide death benefit protection for your beneficiaries. Loans and withdrawals from a permanent or cash value life insurance reduce the policy's cash value and death benefit and increase the chance that the policy may lapse. If the policy lapses, matures, is surrendered, or becomes a modified endowment, the loan balance at such time would generally be viewed as distributed and taxable under the general rules for distributions of policy cash values.

CHAPTER 11:

Types of Life Insurance

SOME PEOPLE DO NOT REALIZE THIS, but there are varied types of life insurance. To ensure that you understand how each type fits into the big picture, let's review them one by one.

Term Insurance

Term life insurance is the most basic type of insurance. It covers the insured for a "term": anywhere from one, 10, 15, 20, or even 30 to 40 years. During the period the insured is covered, and the life insurance company will pay out the death benefit during this timeframe if the insured passes away. However, if the insured dies one day past the term, the beneficiary will receive nothing. All premiums are kept by the life insurance company.

Furthermore, if the insured wants to continue the coverage past the term, the premiums could spike dramatically. For example, we recently looked at a $1 million term policy where the premium went from $448 annually in year 20 to $9,710 annually in year 21.

We should note that there is also something called Annual Renewable Term (ART) in which the premiums start out very low – even lower than, let's say, 20-year term – but increase over time.

In general, term life insurance is relatively inexpensive for younger people.

is tied to a market index (it is not possible to invest directly in an index), as determined by the policy owner. The policyholder then receives a return but with a cap or ceiling on that return, and a floor of zero. So, the policyholder can only benefit in gains up to the cap, which is determined by the life insurance company and can change over the life of the policy. Because of the floor, the policy holder cannot lose money due to market performance but can benefit from market gains. This can make IUL potentially suitable for moderate to conservative investors, based on their individual and unique set of needs and circumstances.

CHAPTER 12:

Variable Universal Life Insurance

THE FINAL TYPE of permanent life insurance is called **variable universal life insurance.** Variable universal life, or VUL, has the same flexible nature of premiums as universal life insurance, but the key difference is how the cash value grows. Rather than being tied to an interest rate, like universal life, or tied to an index, like indexed universal life, VUL allows the client to choose from a selection of different mutual fund investment options. These funds range from conservative to aggressive and from active to passive. In this type of structure, the client is in control of how they want their funds allocated and the risk level they want to take.

Some considerations in buying a VUL include cost, surrender charges, the death benefit, the nature of the flexible premium, and how distributions are made. It is also important to note that this discussion is not intended as a complete description of all the material provisions of variable universal life insurance, as policy features will vary based on the product and its issuing life insurance company.

Variable universal life insurance is offered by prospectus, which contains more complete information about the policy, including risks, charges, expenses, and investment objectives. You should always review the prospectus and consider this information carefully before purchasing a policy.

VUL Costs

The costs of the variable universal life insurance policy, on a percentage of assets basis, is calculated by taking the difference between the gross return of the policy – or the overall pre-fee returns from a policy's investments – and subtract something called the "internal rate of return (IRR) on the net death benefit." This IRR is the return to the owner after all distributions plus the return to the beneficiary upon the insured's death. Assessment and purchase of a policy involves an illustration, or projection of the policy costs and benefits with some assumptions. To fully understand the costs and benefits, make sure that the policy illustration includes what is known as an IRR report, where you can see your percentage cost given the specific policy parameters. Depending on the person and how the policy is structured, there can be a wide range from policy to policy on what the percentage cost it.

John, who is age 35, healthy, and puts the maximum amount into a policy he can, might have an internal percentage cost of less than 1% if he lives to age 90. On the other hand, Martha, who is 65, diabetic, and minimally funds her policy, might have an internal percentage cost of 5% if she lives to 90.

VUL Surrender Charges

One of the downsides of most of this type of policy is the heavy surrender charges in the early years. A surrender charge can be looked at in two similar ways. First, the surrender charge is a fee that the life insurance policyholder is charged upon cancelling their life insurance policy. To understand the second way to think of surrender charges, we first must spell out the difference between the "policy account value" and the "cash surrender value." The policy account value is the value of the cash and securities in the account. The cash surrender value is how much of the policy's cash value the owner of the policy has access to after the surrender charge has been factored in if they decide to surrender (or cancel) the policy.

Permanent life insurance policies typically have surrender charge periods of a certain number of years. During that time, the surrender charge amount decreases annually. For a hypothetical policy, in the first year, the cash surrender value may be only 63% of the policy account value. By year five, the cash surrender value may be up to 96% of the policy account value. By year 10, the policy account value and cash surrender value may be equal, as they will be for the rest of the policy's life.

Keep in mind that different permanent life insurance policies from different life insurance carriers may have varied surrender charge terms and schedules.

Death Benefit

Young couples will want to understand that the IRS has rules about the minimum death benefit allowed to keep the permanent life policy's earnings tax free. The higher the premium amount, the higher the death benefit required. The "face amount" of a life insurance policy is the policy's total net death benefit, or the amount the beneficiary would receive if the insured passed away.

Flexible Nature of Universal Life Insurance Premiums

A common concern of many clients is that if they set out to pay, let's say, a $10,000 annual premium into their policy, what happens if they cannot make that premium payment? This is where the "flexible" nature of the policy premiums come in. Remember that every month, costs are taken out of the cash value to pay for things like administrative fees, cost of insurance, mortality and expense charges, and, if the policy has, a long-term care rider, an additional charge for that rider.

Yet these fees are generally only a relatively small percentage of the premiums. For example, if a policy owner paying a $10,000 annual premium, and hypothetically, only around $1,300 is taken out in costs the first year, those costs are front-loaded into the beginning of the policy. That could at least partially be offset by any potential policy gains that year. If the client does not pay the premium in the second year, only $823 is taken out from the existing cash value (as there is no heavy premium charge). That payment can either be made up from future premiums or be a permanent reduction from the cash value.

In short, the policy can remain in force for a period of time without an additional premium payment, based on the terms of the particular life insurance policy. Note that this is a major difference between all three types of universal life insurance and whole life, term life insurance, and variable life insurance, all of which have fixed premiums. If the premium in those life insurance policy types is not paid when it's due, the policy will lapse.

But what if the client has a permanent issue, due to either lower income or higher expenses, and won't be able to make the $10,000 per year premium at all going forward. Say they might be able to afford only half the amount. Then the death benefit can be lowered to the lowest level possible for that same $5,000 premium, thereby lowering the internal costs in the policy.

Distributions

Given that these policies are set up to maximize the growth of cash value over time tax-free, some policyholders may take distributions from them during their retirement years, though distributions can be made at any time.

Distributions from the cash value of a life insurance policy are technically at first in the form of principal, and then a loan against the policy's death benefit. The death benefit therefore reduces dollar for dollar based on the loan or distribution amount.

The policy's net death benefit reduces as distributions are made, but there still must be some net death benefit left over. The amount and timing of distributions is up to the client.

CHAPTER 13:

Long Term Care

THE NEED FOR LONG-TERM CARE is so often misunderstood. A lot of people think of long-term care as going into a retirement home. Long-term care is actually defined by activities of daily living. There are seven basic activities of daily living:

1. Eating
2. Bathing
3. Dressing
4. Transferring
5. Toileting
6. Walking or Moving Around
7. Mental Cognition

Because of the nature of these activities of daily living, long-term care is usually needed toward the end of one's life. So, while young people usually do not have to worry about long-term care in the near term, about 70% of adults over the age of 65 end up needing to go into long-term care. For young people with aging parents, it is at least a conversation worth having[xxiii]. Many do not think about this because adults over the age of 65 are then eligible for Medicare and surely if this is such a problem, Medicare would cover most of these expenses, right? Wrong.

The burden and costs of long-term care tend to fall on a few different parties: the individual affected, the children of the individual affected, and Medicaid. In 2021, those costs were about $5,000 per month nationwide if the individual was fortunate enough to be able to stay in their own home and about $9,000 per month if they wanted a private room in a facility[xxiv]. According to the National Care Planning Council, the average length of stay in a nursing home is 835 days, which would be about 28 months[xxv]. That 28 months can easily cost over $250,000.

Let us run through a hypothetical scenario. Mom and Dad retire at 65 with Social Security income of $50,000 per year between the two of them and an additional income need of $20,000 after taxes. They retire with $500,000 in various retirement accounts so you as their child feel like they have a pretty good setup to retire comfortably. They reach age 80 and Mom ends up needing round-the-clock care that Dad cannot provide. Mom needs the supervision of a nursing home, and their assets are now $400,000. Because of the care need, their income needs per year went up from $70,000 to $178,000.

Mom luckily does not continue to decline but does continue to need the round-the-clock care. In three years, Mom and Dad's retirement savings are gone. Once their assets dwindle down to $2,000, the state-run program Medicaid kicks in so Mom's care is getting paid for, but Dad can't do any of the things he wanted to be able to in retirement because they have spent all their retirement assets on the care. If you are financially able, you may want to step in and support Dad, maybe even have him live with you.

Because this subject, like death, is not one of the rosier topics, we find that a lot of families are not having these conversations. If you want to have a sound financial plan, it is worth at least discussing what happens before anyone's health starts to decline.

Once people have seen this long-term care expense in action with a loved one or friend, they tend to understand the need and have a deep personal connection. Luckily, there are some ways to plan for these expenses ahead of time.

Self-Insuring

Insurance is meant to reduce risk of a possible scenario causing a financial burden. We are all mandated to have health insurance and car insurance because the cost of not having insurance ends up being an immense burden on those who must shoulder the costs if something happens. You pay premiums for a policy and an insurance company takes on the risk that an unlikely and devastating scenario may happen, and they would be the ones shouldering the financial burden.

If you always have a couple hundred grand in your pocket, perhaps you can foot some or all the cost of a car accident or medical emergency. This is self-insuring.

Self-insuring can make sense for someone who has a lot of excess funds and was a great saver for retirement. If we take that same hypothetical scenario we went through with Mom and Dad, but they had $1.5 million saved for retirement, there may not have been a need for Medicaid or for relying on you as their child.

Medicaid

Medicaid is a welfare program designed to support those who do not have the income to support themselves. Medicaid is the responsibility of the respective state that the person needing care lives in. This basically only becomes an option once all other options have been exhausted. Individuals can maintain a primary residence if it doesn't exceed a certain value, but they generally cannot maintain significant cash or other assets.

Many people want to avoid the need for this option, particularly if there is to be a surviving spouse left after the long-term care need. Having some level of long-term care insurance does provide a measure of protection against the risk of long-term care needs depleting one's assets. If an individual has long-term care coverage that they end up spending down, they are allowed to maintain cash and other assets in an amount equal to the coverage they had. For example, let's say Mom has a $100,000 long-term care policy. While she may be underinsured, it still helps. She can spend down the $100,000 in coverage but maintain $100,000 in personal assets and still qualify for Medicaid since she did make a plan and purchase coverage.

States have also recently put together some legislation to try to reduce the burden of long-term care on their Medicaid system. Washington became the first state in 2019 to pass a payroll tax of 0.58% for all those who do not have existing long-term care coverage[xxvi].

Long Term Care Annuities

Long-term care annuities are one step of leverage above self-insuring. This is built for people who are currently in poor health or might not be able to qualify for traditional long-term care insurance but still want a leveraged benefit. Most of these policies involve putting a lump sum of cash into an annuity that will pay out a higher amount if used for long-term care and basically return what you put in if never used for long-term care. This option involves already having funds to cover at least some of the cost.

Stand-Alone Long Term Care Policies

Long-term care insurance was first introduced in the 1960s[xxvii] and there were many insurance companies that entered the marketplace to offer long-term care insurance to individuals at a very low cost. People would pay a small amount of premiums and if they ever needed care, they would pay for the cost of care upfront and the insurance policy would reimburse them to their costs after an elimination period was satisfied (usually 90 days). Some policies allowed these payments to happen indefinitely.

People who bought these policies tended to value them. They did not want to end up leaving their spouse to suffer financially or burden their children. Business owners and independent contractors also enjoyed that these policy premiums offered some tax deductions and a tax-free benefit on the back end.

Because of these factors, many insurance companies were unable to continue to pay benefits and even successfully petitioned with the insurance department to increase the costs of insurance to existing contract holders. Years later, there are fewer insurance companies issuing stand-alone long-term care policies and the premiums for these policies are much higher than the original long term care policies from the 60s.

Hybrid Policies

Some life insurance companies began offering hybrid life insurance policies that would pre-pay the policy's death benefit to cover long-term care needs. With permanent life insurance, they calculate costs based on the assumption that they will have to pay out the death benefit, so life insurance companies have much more in cash reserves to follow up on their insurance promises. Often, a long-term care event ends in the death of the person needing the care.

For individuals who have a life insurance policy, the spouse and/or the children of the individual needing care would spend their assets on the individual's care. Then, once the individual dies and a death benefit pays out, the spouse and/or children would essentially be reimbursing themselves. This is a bit risky since we do not have a crystal ball and we cannot predict how long someone will need care. Hybrid policies look at this scenario and say, "since we are going to pay you a death benefit anyway, let's take some of the death benefit you would get at the end of life and use it to fund these long-term care expenses."

There are a lot of life insurance companies out there and many have some variation of a long-term care benefit. But if you are considering a hybrid policy for yourself or a loved one, we would urge you to read all the literature to understand how these policies pay out. Many will offer what is known as an indemnity benefit, which is a little different from the stand-alone policies offering a reimbursement benefit. An indemnity benefit will pay an individual their full monthly amount offered by the policy upfront, so they do not need to pay out-of-pocket then submit the receipts for reimbursement every month.

Conclusion

Long-term care is a potentially massive expense that affects many in their retirement years. Long-term care spending is estimated to grow to 3% of gross domestic product in the US by 2050[xxviii] . It is more important now than ever to speak with loved ones about this potential expense and make a plan to manage it.

CHAPTER 14:

Disability Income Insurance

WHILE LONG-TERM CARE INSURANCE is more likely to affect the older generations, disability income insurance may be relevant to you today. Disabilities can be defined in a few different ways by different entities, but the most common way we have seen is something that affects your ability to do the material acts of your work. For example, if you are a realtor and no longer able to drive yourself to house showings, your income is likely to be negatively impacted. If you are a writer and can no longer write, that would also be a problem. Disability income insurance insures a portion of one's income.

Often, if someone is employed by a large company, their work will offer some level of disability income insurance. However, if someone is employed by a smaller business or an independent contractor, they might not have any level of employer-covered disability income insurance.

If you do not have employer-covered disability insurance, you may want to consider getting independent coverage if you fit into one or more of these categories:

- You are the primary breadwinner in your household
- Your expenses are roughly in line with your monthly income
- You do not have sufficient savings to go six months without income

There are a few ways to cover a disability income need. We will go through each of them below.

Self-Insuring

As we have said, we do not have a crystal ball, and so assuming self-insuring will work out is not a perfect system. Self-insuring may be sufficient if you keep six months of expenses in cash and can truly afford to go six months without work. Individuals with a lot of passive income (e.g., rental income, trust income) also may not have a need for disability income insurance, and the income would continue regardless of ability to work. If a disability goes much beyond that, then you may be able to qualify for Social Security disability coverage.

Social Security Disability Insurance (SSDI)

Social Security has a disability income benefit built in. Its definition of disability can be stricter than individual or employer policies. For those who pay into Social Security, income can be payable to someone experiencing a permanent disability. The disability would have to prevent them from being able to do any work in perpetuity, and if they happen to get better, they will need to pay Social Security back.

We once met a woman who was trying to save for retirement but could not scrape together additional funds because of her massive debt to Social Security after being disabled for two years then going back to work.

Social Security's benefits are also capped on the upside. The maximum monthly benefit was $3,627 in 2023, which might be enough for a single person with no children to support, but it would be very difficult to live on for a primary breadwinner or someone with dependents[xxix].

Employer-Paid Disability Income Insurance

Many who work for large companies get to enjoy the luxury of insurance coverage they have never had to think about before. Employers will often offer both short-term disability income insurance and long-term disability income insurance. Short-term often replaces a percentage of your income for the first 90 days of a disability, and long-term often replaces a percentage of your income for beyond the 90 days up to the policy limit. Usually, for short-term disability, we will look at whether a person can do their own job or if there is something that prevents them from being able to do that job.

We once had an office in a city where our receptionist rode her motorbike into the office every day. One weekend, she had a fall and broke her leg. So, her doctor said that she was no longer able to commute into work for the time being and she was able to receive short-term disability until she was recovered.

For long-term disability, we look at whether that person can perform their job functions over a long period of time. An injury would still apply here if the recovery time went beyond three months. For example, let's say a researcher suddenly has constant migraines affecting her ability to draw conclusions from her research for a long period of time. Her doctor cannot figure out a solution to the problem right now, but since she cannot do her work, she needs income replacement.

Long-term disability can also vary a lot in the time range offered. Employer coverage may be one to five years, depending on the employee benefit offered. On the longer end, some policies can pay residual disability income benefits in perpetuity. It is important to understand your employer-paid disability income coverage if you want to make sure you and your family would be financially secure in the event of a disability.

Independent Insurance

Many insurance policies will have small differences but generally with independent insurance, the definition for disability includes loss of time dedicated to the material acts of your work. As an example, if the loss of time is 20% or greater, the policy might go into effect, depending on the terms of the disability income insurance policy. A policyholder might get 60% of their average earned income replaced up to $35,000 per month, again depending on the terms of the policy. People often seek out long-term disability coverage when gaining access to independent coverage because short-term disability can be quite cost-prohibitive.

We would like to go into the example of a temporary disability in this case. Let's say that you run a small business and get cancer. The doctor tells you that it is entirely treatable, and you will most likely recover over the next year, but you will need to come in for radiation treatment once per week on Fridays. Out of a five-day work week, you are losing 20% of your time dedicated to running that business. With fatigue from radiation, your productivity may be hit even harder and result in a 40% loss of income. Maybe you even need to hire another person to take on some of your duties for the time being. In that time, the disability policy pays for some of that lost income, and once you are completely cancer-free and recovered, you are not in such a financial hole and the business was able to continue.

Unfortunately, it can be very difficult for someone who is new to their occupation to gain independent coverage because financial underwriting is often required for gaining coverage. An individual must prove that their income levels are what they claim in order to gain disability income insurance coverage for that income level.

Individuals who have received consistent income for the last two years in their occupation, do not have employer-covered disability income insurance, and the household is reliant on their income can often be best suited for income replacement through independent disability income insurance.

Independent policies generally range in the length of coverage. People can get one or five years of coverage like the employer plans, but these policies can even stretch to an assumed retirement age of 65 or older. In that case, if a 45-year-old becomes disabled and has the maximum coverage they can get, they might receive 20 years of income replacement up to a percentage of their earned income, depending on the disability income insurance policy they own. Independent policies can also offer additional coverage in the event of a total disability, which would include loss of sight, hearing, or use of two or more limbs.

PART 4:
The Value of an Advisor

CHAPTER 15:

Should You Work with a Financial Professional?

As you navigate your financial life, one of the decisions you'll have to make is whether to work with a financial professional.

One of the best analogies Dan likes to give for working with a financial professional is that, in some ways, it can be like going to a personal trainer. Sure, you can work out on your own, but the trainer provides an acute focus to improve your fitness outcome based on your goals and abilities. Perhaps even more importantly, a trainer can help with discipline and accountability. In the same way, financial professionals not only use their professional focus and experience to help you identify suitable and appropriate products and services to address your financial goals, but they can also help you stay on track as your circumstances, needs, and goals change over time.

As financial professionals, we're obviously big fans of working with our profession.

Let's look more specifically at some of the things financial professionals can do to help their clients. To begin with, the simple yet too often ignored foundation of financial planning is to create a financial strategy. From an investing perspective, this may include behavioral coaching, asset allocation, rebalancing, and asset location (or putting assets in the appropriate tax buckets). From a risk management perspective, licensed financial professionals can offer the right types of life insurance needs analysis, offer suitable life and disability income, and long-term care insurance.

Financial Needs Analysis: At its root, financial analysis begins with taking an inventory of a client's financial picture, to include their income and earnings, assets and liabilities, and expenses. It then determines what their goals are and what they need to do to accomplish these goals. Goals can include retirement planning, estate planning and leaving a legacy, education planning, major purchase planning, and even tax efficiency analysis.

Behavioral Coaching: Behavioral coaching is helping clients adhere to their long-term financial plan so they can stay on track toward their goals when their emotions tell them otherwise. According to Vanguard, "advisors, as behavioral coaches, can act as emotional circuit breakers by circumventing clients' tendencies to chase returns or run for cover in emotionally charged markets. In the process, advisors may save their clients from significant wealth destruction and also add percentage points— rather than basis points—of value."[xxx]

Correct Asset Allocation: Asset allocation, as discussed earlier, is the proportion of a portfolio's investments in different asset classes, such as stocks, bonds, real estate, cash, alternative investments, etc. It is critical, and the fundamental belief of our investment management philosophy, that clients' asset allocation be based on their risk tolerance. Therefore, helping clients use their risk tolerance to determine how allocate their assets is a key role that financial professionals play. But keep in mind that asset allocation does not guarantee a profit or protection against investment losses in a declining market.

Rebalancing: Say we do help our client set up an asset allocation that is appropriately based on the client's financial needs analysis, and it's determined that the client should be in roughly 60% stocks and 40% bonds. What happens if stocks start advancing and bonds decline, so that at the end of the year our portfolio is now 65% stocks and only 35% bonds. Rebalancing by selling some stocks and then buying some bonds to get the portfolio back to the 60/40 allocation may be necessary. Some people may not regularly rebalance their portfolio unless they're working with a financial professional. As with asset allocation, portfolio rebalancing does not guarantee a profit or protection against investment losses in a declining market.

Asset Location: While we've discussed asset allocation at length, asset location is determining where assets might be placed based on how they are taxed. There are essentially three buckets for tax treatment: pre-tax, taxable, and tax-free.

Pre-tax: This includes traditional IRAs, 401(k)s, and 403(b)s where you receive the tax deduction at time of contribution, do not pay taxes as the money grows, but then must pay taxes at distribution.

Taxable: This includes regular brokerage accounts where money is taxed as it's earned before investing, as it potentially grows, and at distribution.

Tax-Free: This includes qualified Roth IRA distributions (Roth IRA contributions are not tax deductible), some municipal securities, properly structured life insurance, and 529 plans where contributions are not tax deductible, and earnings are federal income tax-free and generally state income tax-free when they are used for qualified education expenses.

Helping You Decide on Insurance Products: There are literally thousands of companies and products in the life insurance, disability income insurance, and long-term care insurance space. In addition to helping determine your need for these types of insurance, a duly licensed financial professional with knowledge of these types of products can help guide you to find one specific to your needs.

Academic Evidence

While we cited many studies from professional sources, we thought we'd cite some studies from academic sources as well.

In "Good Advice, Good Outcomes," published in the Social Science Research Network, the authors find that "financial advising is associated with improved financial behavior and well-being for non-retired persons."[xxxi]

In "Financial Advice and Individual Investor Portfolio Performance," "the findings indicate that portfolios of advised investors are better diversified and carry significantly less idiosyncratic risk."[xxxii]

But Do You Really *Need* a Financial Professional?

Of course, despite all the evidence for our value, it's true that you do not need a financial professional to invest your own money. But you will often need a properly licensed agent or broker to buy permanent life insurance, disability income insurance, or long-term care insurance.

Essentially anyone can access and use an online brokerage account.

So, you might not find a need for a financial professional if …

1) You have determined, and quantified, your financial goals.
2) You have evaluated your risk tolerance for each of your financial goals.
3) You have allocated your portfolios in accordance with the risk tolerance for each of those financial goals.
4) You've never changed your allocation when panicked (think March 2020, Sept/Oct 2018, or October 2008).
5) You rebalance your retirement accounts quarterly (or more often) as needed, and taxable accounts once a year.
6) You know where to locate your assets among accounts with different tax treatment.
7) You're clear on the considerations for withdrawal order from accounts with different tax treatments.

But if you haven't done *all* those things, it might make sense to speak to a financial professional. In the end it will all come down to whether you feel the need to get professional financial services.

References

[i] https://www.forbes.com/sites/dandoonan/2021/07/30/high-retirement-anxiety-for-millennials-and-generation-x/?sh=41ba50386535
[ii] https://u.demog.berkeley.edu/~andrew/1918/figure2.html
[iii] https://www.worldometers.info/demographics/life-expectancy/
[iv] https://www.ssa.gov/benefits/retirement/planner/agereduction.html)
[v] https://www.aarp.org/retirement/social-security/questions-answers/how-much-longer-will-social-security-be-around.html
[vi] https://www.ssa.gov/policy/docs/ssb/v70n3/v70n3p111.html
[vii] https://www.ssa.gov/policy/docs/ssb/v69n3/v69n3p1.html
[viii] https://www.statista.com/statistics/797321/us-population-by-generation/
[ix] https://www.cfainstitute.org/en/research/foundation/2021/sbbi-2021-summary-edition
[x] https://educationdata.org/average-cost-of-college#:~:text=The%20average%20cost%20of%20college,annual%20growth%20rate%20of%206.8%25
[xi] https://educationdata.org/student-loan-debt-statistics
[xii] https://www.spglobal.com/spdji/en/indices/indicators/sp-corelogic-case-shiller-us-national-home-price-nsa-index/#overview
[xiii] https://www.investopedia.com/ask/answers/042415/what-average-annual-return-sp-500.asp
[xiv] https://www.multpl.com/case-shiller-home-price-index-inflation-adjusted
[xv] https://www.bankrate.com/real-estate/homebuyer-regret-survey-may-2021/
[xvi] For examples of portfolio allocations based on years until retirement see Burton Malkiel, *A Random Walk Down Wall Street: The Time Tested Strategy for Successful Investing* (New York: W.W. Norton and Company), p. 346-347, John Bogle, *Common Sense on Mutual Funds* (Hoboken, New Jersey: John Wiley & Sons, 2010.), p. 84, and David Swensen, *Unconventional Success: A Fundamental Approach to Personal Investment* (New York: The Free Press, 2005), p. 87-90.
[xvii] https://my.dimensional.com/asset/577/performance-of-the-premiums
[xviii] For a discussion of Prospect Theory see Daniel Kahneman, *Thinking, Fast and Slow* (New York: Farrar, Straus and Giroux, 2011), p. 278- 288.
[xix] Robert Shiller, *Irrational Exuberance: Revised and Expanded Third Edition* (Princeton and Oxford: Princeton University Press, 2015), p. 106.
[xx] Shiller, 107
[xxi] Shiller, 104.
[xxii] Meir Statman, *Finance for Normal People (*New York: Oxford University Press, 2017), p. 47.
[xxiii] https://acl.gov/ltc/basic-needs/how-much-care-will-you-need#:~:text=Someone%20turning%20age%2065%20today,)%20than%20men%20(2.2%20years)

[xxiv] https://www.genworth.com/aging-and-you/finances/cost-of-care.html.
[xxv] https://www.ahcancal.org/Assisted-Living/Facts-and-Figures/Pages/default.aspx
[xxvi] https://wacaresfund.wa.gov/private-insurance/
[xxvii] https://content.naic.org/cipr-topics/long-term-care-insurance
[xxviii] https://content.naic.org/cipr-topics/long-term-care-insurance).
[xxix] Social Security chrome-extension://efaidnbmnnnibpcajpcglclefindmkaj/https://www.ssa.gov/news/press/factsheets/colafacts2023.pdf
[xxx] Vanguard, Putting a Value on Your Value, p.17
[xxxi] Schmeiser, Maximilian D. and Hogarth, Jeanne M., Good Advice, Good Outcomes? How Financial Advice-Seeking Relates to Self-Perceived Financial Well-Being (May 7, 2013). Available at SSRN: https://ssrn.com/abstract=2261707 or http://dx.doi.org/10.2139/ssrn.2261707
[xxxii] Kramer, Marc, Financial Advice and Individual Investor Portfolio Performance (December 9, 2011). Financial Management, 2012, Available at SSRN: https://ssrn.com/abstract=1970250

Made in the USA
Monee, IL
04 November 2026

67380875R00049